BATTLE OF THE BEAUTIES

FRIGGA
VS
APHRODITE

by Lydia Lukidis

a Capstone company — publishers for children

Raintree is an imprint of Capstone Global Library Limited, a company incorporated in England and Wales having its registered office at 264 Banbury Road, Oxford, OX2 7DY – Registered company number: 6695582

www.raintree.co.uk
myorders@raintree.co.uk

Hardback edition © Capstone Global Library Limited 2024
Paperback edition © Capstone Global Library Limited 2025
The moral rights of the proprietor have been asserted.

All rights reserved. No part of this publication may be reproduced in any form or by any means (including photocopying or storing it in any medium by electronic means and whether or not transiently or incidentally to some other use of this publication) without the written permission of the copyright owner, except in accordance with the provisions of the Copyright, Designs and Patents Act 1988 or under the terms of a licence issued by the Copyright Licensing Agency, 5th Floor, Shackleton House, 4 Battle Bridge Lane, London SE1 2HX (www.cla.co.uk). Applications for the copyright owner's written permission should be addressed to the publisher.

Edited by Aaron Sautter
Designed by Bobbie Nuytten
Original illustrations © Capstone Global Library Limited 2024
Picture research by Rebekah Hubstenberger
Production by Whitney Schaefer
Originated by Capstone Global Library Ltd
Printed and bound in India

978 1 3982 5268 4 (hardback)
978 1 3982 5269 1 (paperback)

British Library Cataloguing in Publication Data
A full catalogue record for this book is available from the British Library.

Acknowledgements
We would like to thank the following for permission to reproduce photographs: Alamy: Chronicle, 7, 17, 19, 25, Historic Images, 27, Lebrecht Music & Arts, 4, SPCOLLECTION; 15, Bridgeman Images: 11; Dreamstime: Volodymyr Polotovskyi, 8; Getty Images: Aleksej Arestov/EyeEm, 22, Grafissimo, 23, iStock/LeniKovaleva, 9, Photos.com, 21, iStock/Stanislav Chegleev, cover (bottom right), 5, 29; Shutterstock: Prokrida, cover (top left), 28, Ruslana Stovner, 13; The Metropolitan Museum of Art: The Elisha Whittelsey Collection, The Elisha Whittelsey Fund, 1966, 12

Every effort has been made to contact copyright holders of material reproduced in this book. Any omissions will be rectified in subsequent printings if notice is given to the publisher.

All the internet addresses (URLs) given in this book were valid at the time of going to press. However, due to the dynamic nature of the internet, some addresses may have changed, or sites may have changed or ceased to exist since publication. While the author and publisher regret any inconvenience this may cause readers, no responsibility for any such changes can be accepted by either the author or the publisher.

CONTENTS

The queen vs the Olympian 4
Divine beginnings 6
Incredible strengths 10
Awesome powers 18
Flawed goddesses 24
Frigga vs Aphrodite at a glance 28
Glossary 30
Find out more 31
Index 32
About the author 32

Words in **bold** are in the glossary.

THE QUEEN VS THE OLYMPIAN

A light mist hovers above the ground. A woman sits on a throne, holding a commanding pose. She wears a long robe the colour of the sky.

All hail Frigga! She's the most important goddess of the Norse **pantheon**. She is a mighty queen who rules beside her husband, Odin, the Allfather.

Frigga is the goddess of motherhood and running a household. But her duties don't end there. She's also in charge of marriage, childbirth and **fertility**.

Frigga

FACT

There are many similarities between the Norse goddesses Frigga and Freya. In fact, some historians believe they are the same goddess.

CHIRP, CHIRP!

A dozen sparrows whoosh through the air, lugging a chariot. A beautiful goddess steers it.

Welcome, Aphrodite! She's one of the twelve **Olympians** in Greek mythology. Aphrodite is a very busy goddess. She's in charge of love and beauty, fertility, marriage and **procreation**. She also has a special connection to the sea.

Aphrodite is very graceful, but she's also tough. She has both a kind and a destructive side.

Which of these gifted goddesses is more powerful? Who has more abilities? Frigga and Aphrodite will have to battle it out. Who will come out on top?

Aphrodite

DIVINE BEGINNINGS

Frigga is a mysterious goddess. We don't know much about her origins. Historians aren't even sure who her family is.

Some ancient Norse texts say she's the daughter of Fjorgynn – a male giant with godly powers. He represents the earth. Like Odin, Frigga probably comes from a line of giants. In Norse mythology, the giants were the first beings. They existed even before the gods.

As for Frigga's mother, nobody really knows who she is. But we do know that Frigga's name means "beloved" or "dear".

The giant Ymir was the first being to appear in Norse mythology. The race of giants was born from his body.

Venus

FACT

The Birth of Venus is a famous painting that artist Sandro Botticelli created in 1485. The Roman goddess Venus is based on Aphrodite, so this painting also references Aphrodite.

How did Aphrodite come to be? Actually, there are two stories about her birth. The first is fairly normal. In Greek myths, her father is Zeus, king of the gods. Her mother is Dione, an ancient **Titaness**. This makes Aphrodite a second-generation goddess, like most Olympians.

But the Greek poet Hesiod weaves a more incredible tale. He says Aphrodite's birth began with the titan Cronus. Cronus wanted to be in charge, so he killed his father, Uranus. According to the myths, Uranus was the original god of the heavens.

Then, SPLOOSH! Cronus tossed Uranus's body into the sea. Then a foam began to appear in the water and a scallop shell rose up from the foam. Aphrodite then emerged from the shell wearing no clothes. The story fits. After all, the Greek word *aphros* means "sea foam".

One story says Aphrodite first appeared from the ocean riding on a large seashell.

INCREDIBLE STRENGTHS

Frigga has many strengths. She's best known for her fierce dedication as a loving mother. Mothers give life and unconditional love.

Frigga has two children: twin sons Baldur and Hodr. She would do anything for them. One famous Norse tale shows her devotion. One night, Baldur had a nightmare that predicted his death. Frigga had the same nightmare. But she was determined to prevent her son's death.

She used her powers and authority to make all things in creation, living and non-living, promise to never harm her son. She visited giants and gods. She talked to animals and plants. She even made elements and objects such as fire, water, stones and weapons promise her son's safety. Unfortunately, Baldur died anyway. But Frigga never gave up trying to save him.

Frigga called on all living and non-living things to protect her son Baldur.

Aphrodite's main strength can be summed up in one word: love. As the goddess of love, countless gods and **mortal** men admire her. With just one glance, she can make others fall head over heels for her.

But she's not just incredibly beautiful. She also owns a magical **girdle**. It makes the person wearing it irresistible. She can make others fall in love and desire one another too. For example, she helped spark the love between the Greek hero Jason and Medea, the daughter of the Colchian King.

Neither the gods nor mortal men could resist Aphrodite's beauty.

Aphrodite isn't just the goddess of love and desire. She also oversees marriage, fertility and childbirth. She brings others together to create a strong family.

FACT

Aphrodite's son Eros is also in charge of love. Eros is a god but looks more like a young boy with wings. He's similar to Cupid from Roman mythology.

Eros

Frigga isn't just a loving mother. She has many other strengths. Intelligence? Check. A strong will and an independent spirit? Check and check. She's a supportive wife to Odin, too. But make no mistake, she's not his servant. She's his equal.

In Norse myths, Frigga is the only person other than Odin allowed to sit on his throne. And, even though Odin is the Norse god of wisdom, Frigga can outsmart him. In one tale, Frigga and Odin bet on which prince will make a better King, Agnar or Geirröth. Frigga outwitted her husband and won.

Like Aphrodite, Frigga is also a goddess of fertility and marriage. She often arranges marriages and protects families. She also helps women in childbirth. In one ancient poem, Frigga uses special plants and herbs to help women have their babies.

Marshland queen

In Norse mythology, Frigga is very independent. In fact, she doesn't always live with her husband, Odin. She often stays in the foggy, watery realm of Fensalir, which means "hall of the marshlands". All marshy and swampy grounds are special to Frigga.

Love isn't Aphrodite's only power. Her other main strength is her stunning beauty. Thanks to her perfect body and face, she enchants all those who look her way. She also has the power to grant beauty and charms to others.

Beauty may not seem very powerful, but think again. Because of her beauty, Aphrodite can influence others. In a famous myth, Zeus asked Paris, a mortal man, to decide who was the most beautiful – Aphrodite, Hera or Athena. Of course, Aphrodite won.

Before Paris picked Aphrodite in the beauty contest, she had promised him the love of the most beautiful mortal woman, Helen. But Helen was married to King Menelaus of Sparta. Aphrodite helped Paris kidnap Helen and take her to Troy. Her actions helped spark the Trojan War.

Paris chose Aphrodite as the most beautiful of all the goddesses.

AWESOME POWERS

Like Odin, Frigga has certain powers when it comes to magic. In an ancient manuscript found in Germany, Frigga is shown using magic to heal a horse.

Frigga also has the power of **divination**. She can see into the future. Before Baldur died, she had a vivid dream that predicted his death.

As a sky goddess and master weaver, Frigga weaves the clouds that produce rain to help crops grow. She also weaves the magical threads of fate, known as *Wyrd*, in a similar way.

FACT

Frigga first appeared in Marvel comics as Thor's mother, and Loki's adoptive mother, in 1963. She was later an important part of the first two Thor films.

Spin master

As a homemaker, Frigga takes pride in her skill at spinning wool. In many myths, she uses the wool of the cloud sheep to weave and spin garments for the gods. Many women call on her when they need help spinning wool. As a goddess of the sky, Frigga also spins and weaves the clouds themselves.

Step aside, Frigga! You're not the only powerful one. Aphrodite also has great power – the power of creation. Pygmalion was a famous sculptor. He created a statue of a woman so beautiful that he fell in love with it. He begged Aphrodite to turn the statue into a real woman. Aphrodite agreed, then, POOF! She brought the statue to life.

Aphrodite also played a role in the creation of the first mortal woman, Pandora. The gods formed Pandora out of clay. Then Aphrodite gifted her with beauty that made her powerful and desired by others.

Aphrodite can even help protect her favourite warriors. She saved Paris when he was about to be killed during the Trojan War. She wrapped him in a cloud that carried him home to safety.

Pandora

FACT

The character of Aphrodite often appeared in the TV series *Hercules: The Legendary Journeys* and *Xena: Warrior Princess*. She also featured in the Percy Jackson and the Olympians series written by Rick Riordan.

Aphrodite has another handy superpower – immortality. This goddess will live forever. As for Frigga, her fate is unclear. Many Norse gods will die during Ragnarök. At this final battle nearly all mortal people and gods will die.

But Frigga and Aphrodite do have one other power in common: the ability to **shapeshift**. Frigga can turn herself into a bird using a pair of magical falcon **plumes**.

Frigga's magical feathers gave her the ability to take the form of a bird.

Aphrodite can take the form of various creatures. In one myth, the monster Typhon descended upon Mount Olympus. He threatened to attack the gods and goddesses. As he approached Aphrodite, she escaped by turning herself into a fish.

When necessary, Aphrodite could turn into creatures such as fish.

FLAWED GODDESSES

Although Frigga is powerful and a devoted mother, she can't save Baldur. Loki, a trickster god in Norse mythology, tricked her. Frigga had asked everything in creation to help protect Baldur. However, she didn't ask the mistletoe plant. She thought it was small and harmless. But Loki discovered this and made a spear from mistletoe.

Because Frigga had made everything promise to protect her son, Baldur seemed to be **invincible**. Nothing could harm him. One day, the gods decided to test this by throwing weapons at Baldur. However, Loki told the blind god Hodr to hurl the mistletoe spear at Baldur. It killed him instantly. Baldur was trapped in the underworld forever, and Frigga was overcome with sadness.

Despite her efforts, Frigga was unable to save Baldur's life.

Frigga isn't always wise and powerful. She can also be sneaky and dishonest. In some Norse myths, she enjoys tricking her husband.

Aphrodite is the most beautiful of all the Greek goddesses. However, she's not always very nice. She can be **spiteful** and arrogant. Many Greek myths show her punishing those who don't worship her.

The women living on the island of Lemnos are a great example. They refused to honour Aphrodite. So she made them smell so bad that their husbands couldn't stand to be near them!

Aphrodite also isn't loyal to her husband, Hephaestus. She has more than twelve children, but guess what? Hephaestus isn't the father of any of them. Aphrodite has many other boyfriends, both gods and mortal men. She tends to cause chaos wherever she goes. For example, she caused a lot of fighting between the gods on Mount Olympus. Why? Because she had relationships with almost all of the Olympians except Zeus and Hades.

Both Frigga and Aphrodite have strengths, powers and weaknesses. Who do you think is the greater goddess?

Petty and jealous

Aphrodite is very jealous. There was once a beautiful mortal woman called Psyche. Aphrodite became jealous of her beauty. One day, she told Eros to use his golden arrows on Psyche. Aphrodite wanted Psyche to fall in love with the ugliest man on Earth. But the plan backfired. Eros was nicked by the arrow and fell in love with Psyche instead.

Psyche and Eros

FRIGGA VS APHRODITE AT A GLANCE

Name:	Frigga
Goddess of:	motherhood, marriage, household management, weaving, childbirth, family, fertility, the sky and prophecy
Appearance:	motherly figure dressed in a robe, often blue to symbolise the sky, with young fair skin and long, dark blonde hair
Weapons:	magic and sometimes a staff
Strengths:	dedicated as a loving mother, intelligent, wise, strong will, independent spirit, helps with marriage, family and childbirth
Powers and abilities:	magic, witchcraft, uses magical herbs for healing, power of divination, clever, able to shapeshift
Weaknesses:	her power and authority have limits (she's couldn't save her son), can be dishonest and sneaky
Symbols:	spinning wheel, spindle, mistletoe, the sky

Name:	Aphrodite
Goddess of:	love, beauty, pleasure, fertility, marriage and procreation
Appearance:	young beautiful woman with long, light-brown hair, perfect body, beautiful flowing clothes and jewellery
Weapons:	beauty and a magical girdle
Strengths:	power of love for herself and others, irresistible, helps marriages and families, stunning beauty
Powers and abilities:	power of creation, able to protect her favourite warriors, immortal, able to shapeshift
Weaknesses:	spiteful, arrogant, holds a grudge, disloyal, dishonest and jealous
Symbol:	scallop shell, girdle, dove, sparrows

GLOSSARY

divination see into and have knowledge of the future

fertility ability to have a child; ability of the land to grow crops

girdle belt or sash worn around the waist

invincible unable to be injured or killed

mortal one who has a limited lifespan and eventually dies

Olympian main gods and goddesses in Greek mythology who lived on Mount Olympus

pantheon all the gods of a certain mythology

plume long and fluffy feather or group of feathers

procreation act or process of producing babies

shapeshift ability to transform into another form, such as a person, animal or creature

spiteful treat others in a mean or unpleasant way

Titaness female giant that was a goddess of ancient Greece before the Olympians took over

FIND OUT MORE

BOOKS

The Ancient Greeks (Analysing Ancient Civilizations), Louise Spilsbury (Raintree, 2019)

The Book of Mythical Beasts and Magical Creatures: Meet your favourite monsters, fairies, heroes and tricksters from all around the world, Stephen Krensky (DK Children, 2020)

Norse Myths, Matt Ralphs (DK Children, 2021)

WEBSITES

www.bbc.co.uk/bitesize/topics/zx339j6/articles/ztxwsrd
Learn more about myths and legends.

www.dkfindout.com/uk/history/ancient-greece/ancient-greek-gods-and-goddesses
Find out more about the ancient Greek gods and goddesses.

www.dkfindout.com/uk/history/vikings/viking-gods
Find out more about Viking gods.

INDEX

Baldur 10, 11, 18, 24, 25
beauty 12, 16, 26, 29

disloyalty 26, 29

Eros 13, 27

fertility 4, 5, 13, 14, 28, 29
films and TV series 18, 21
Freya 4

giants 6, 7, 10

Hephaestus 26
Hesiod 9
Hodr 10, 24

immortality 22, 29
intelligence 14, 28

jealousy 27, 29

Loki 24
love 12, 16, 29

magic 12, 18, 28, 29
marriage 4, 5, 13, 14, 28, 29
motherhood 10, 14, 28

Odin 4, 6, 14, 15, 18
origin myths 6, 8–9

Pandora 20, 21
Paris 16, 17, 20
power of creation 20–21, 29

Ragnarök 22

shapeshifting 22–23, 28, 29

Trojan War 16, 20

Venus 8

Zeus 8, 16, 26

ABOUT THE AUTHOR

Lydia Lukidis is passionate about science, the ocean and mythology. She's the author of more than 50 trade and educational books, as well as 31 ebooks. She loves writing STEM titles, such as *Deep, Deep, Down: The Secret Underwater Poetry of the Mariana Trench* (Raintree, 2023) and *The Broken Bees' Nest* (Kane Press, 2019), which was nominated for a Cybils Award. Lydia also helps foster children's literacy and offers writing workshops and author visits in primary schools.